NEWTOWN PUBLIC LIBRARY
3544 WEST CHESTER PIKE
NEWTOWN SQUARE, PENNA. 19073

Acknowledgments
Translated by Jane Sutton
The publishers would like to thank Jean Imrie
for her help and advice.
Nature consultant for the German edition,
Una Jacobs.

Library of Congress Cataloging-in-Publication Data

Jacobs, Una.
    Earth calendar.

    Translation of: Die Erd-Uhr.
    Includes index.
    1. Seasons — Juvenile literature.   I. Title.
QH81.J2413   1986   574.5′43   85-43557
ISBN 0-382-09216-3
ISBN 0-382-09219-8 (pbk.)

First published 1985 Verlag Heinrich Ellermann,
München with the title *Die Erd-Uhr*
© 1985 Verlag Heinrich Ellermann, München

English translation © 1985 A & C Black (Publishers)
Limited.

Adapted and published in the
United States in 1986 by
Silver Burdett Company,
Morristown, New Jersey

Printed in West Germany

Contents

Earth Calendar

Written and illustrated by Una Jacobs

Silver Burdett Company, Morristown, New Jersey

The Earth

Traveling through space are a countless number of stars and planets. But the Earth is different from these planets because we know there are people, animals, and plants living here.

The Earth is one of nine planets which all travel around the same sun. The Earth takes a year to complete its journey around the sun. During this journey we have spring, summer, autumn, and winter.

As the Earth travels through space it spins around. It takes 24 hours for the Earth to turn around completely. This gives us day and night. At night we can see our nearest neighbor in space, the moon. It travels around the planet Earth as the Earth moves around the sun.

The Earth is surrounded by a thick layer of gases called the **atmosphere**. This protects the Earth from the direct heat of the sun's rays. Otherwise all the things living on the Earth would burn up. The atmosphere also stops heat from escaping from the Earth too quickly.

A strong force radiates from the Earth like a magnet. This is the Earth's **gravity**. Gravity holds everything firmly on Earth so that nothing is flung into space as the Earth spins.

The area around the North Pole is called the Arctic. The huge Arctic Ocean is here. On the ice floes and coasts of the northern countries, polar bears, seals, and seabirds live.

North Pole

The sun's rays reaching the North Pole

The sun's rays reaching the equator

In the tropical areas of the African continent it is hot all year round. Dense forests grow here. In the dry areas there are giraffes, elephants, lions, long tailed monkeys, and lots of other animals. In some parts of the continent there is almost no rain and the land has become a scorching desert.

The sun's rays reaching the South Pole

At the South Pole, in the Antarctic, the snow and ice never melt. They tower many feet high above the land. Only penguins and other animals that can live in the cold can be found here.

South Pole

The European and North American continents lie in the temperate zone where there are warm summers and cold winters. This book looks at the animals and plants that live and grow there.

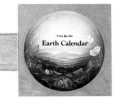

The Earth's Climate

The Earth's surface is made up of land and water. Four great oceans cover seventy percent of the Earth. There are seven big land masses called **continents**. In this picture are Asia, Antarctica, Africa, and Europe. North and South America and Australia are on the other side of the globe.

Because the Earth is round, the sun's rays reach the Earth at an angle. At the North Pole and the South Pole the rays are spread over a wide area so it is very cold. These are the icy **polar** regions.

The farther away you travel from the Poles, the warmer or more **temperate** it becomes. At the equator the sun's rays burn down vertically. This is the hot **tropical** zone.

The strength of the sun's rays is an important part of the climate of a place. So are the wind and rain. The climate also depends on how far inland a place is, or how high it is above sea level, or whether it is sheltered by the mountains or exposed to the sea winds. Every place has its own animal and plant life which has adapted over a long time to the climate there. The area we will be looking at lies in the temperate zone.

The Earth's Crust

The center of the Earth is thousands of miles beneath our feet. Deep inside the Earth is a red-hot mass of liquid rock and metal. On the outside of this fireball a firm, wrinkled skin has formed where the rock has cooled. This is the Earth's **crust**. The wrinkles in the crust are the mountains, valleys, plains, and the sea bed.

All around us, on land, in the air, and in the water, there are plants and animals. But high in the mountains, 9,000 feet above sea level, the air is too cold for anything to live and grow. And the sun's rays can't reach deep into the sea, below 500 feet, so hardly anything lives here.

That leaves a very small part of the Earth for animals and plants to live and grow on. There are 4 billion people and millions of different animals and plants. They all have to share the small space on Earth where there is enough light and warmth to live.

The Landscape

The mountains, valleys, and plains have not always been where they are now. A long time ago, during the Ice Age, it was very cold on Earth. For thousands of years snow and ice piled up in huge **glaciers** over the northern part of the globe.

These glaciers crept down the mountains like rivers of ice. As they moved over the land, they ground down rocks, scraped out valleys and pushed boulders along in front of them. When the Earth's climate grew warmer, most of the ice melted away, leaving behind the landscape we see today.

But the landscape also changes with the seasons. Each season covers the countryside in different colors. In the spring, the countryside is green, the summer adds brightly colored flowers, and in the autumn, the leaves turn brown and orange. Now it is winter and the countryside lies under a blanket of snow.

Erosion

There are other changes going on that happen so gradually that we don't notice them. Wind and water both change the shape of our landscape. As ocean waves are blown against the coastline, the water wears away the land. Melting snow and rain dissolve tiny parts of the soil and carry them away. Torrential streams and rivers carry earth and gravel from the mountains and deposit them on the coast or in the sea. This is called **erosion** and it has been happening for thousands of years.

But inside the Earth, the molten rock and metal push against the Earth's crust. Where the crust is thin or weak, there may be a volcanic eruption, earthquake, or landslide. Sometimes new mountains are formed. These remind us that the Earth's landscape is changing all the time.

Rocks and Soil

Have you ever collected stones or pebbles because you liked the color of them or the way they sparkled? Stones are made up of different **minerals**. These give the stones their different colors.

The rocks in the top picture are very hard. For millions of years, the sun, rain, wind, and snow have passed over them. Heat has expanded the rock and cold has contracted the rock until it has cracked. Rain and snow seep into the cracks in the rock. In frosty weather the water expands to turn into ice and breaks up the rock.

Gradually lichens (1) settle there. They take the minerals which they need from the rock and help to wear it down. Later, the first mossy cushions and other plants (2) grow in the cracks. Air and water fill the small holes between the crumbs of earth.

The hard rock is weathered for many thousands of years until it crumbles into small stones, sand, and fine clay. All these are made up of different minerals. Together with bits of dead plants and animals they make up the soil. And don't forget that the tiny animals living in the soil are also part of it (3).

Earth can be made up of many different things, so there are different types of soil. Loam, for example, is a mixture of decayed plants, clay, and sand. This type of soil is very fertile, so plants can grow easily.

If you look a few feet down into the earth in a quarry or excavation, you can usually see layers of different colors and thicknesses.

At the top of the earth (1) you can see the dark brown **topsoil**. Under that is the paler, rocky **subsoil** (2). The rock here is constantly worn down by the water seeping through the soil. So new minerals mix in with the soil already there. The topsoil and subsoil can be several feet deep or just a few inches. In these two layers of soil there are animals living and plants growing. Under the soil there is rock (3), so nothing can live there.

When the snow melts or the rain falls, water seeps into the soil. Very fine soils which are mostly clay, hold the water. They become saturated like a wet sponge. The water can run quickly through light, sandy soils. It makes its way farther downward through the cracks and through the tiny holes in **porous** rock. Sometimes the water meets limestone. The limestone dissolves easily in water and is carried away. After many years this may leave a hollow in the limestone and form a cave.

Finally, the water meets a layer of nonporous rock (5) which won't let the water through. The water collects there as an underground pool (4). It flows toward the sea as an underground stream.

Underground water can be valuable drinking water for us because it is usually clear and clean. On its long journey through the soil and porous rock the water is filtered and purified, as though it has been through a sieve.

But rainwater can also carry harmful substances into the soil. Exhaust fumes and oil from cars, or poisons from dumps and factories can be dissolved in rain water and carried through the soil. Then the soil becomes polluted and the underground water is undrinkable.

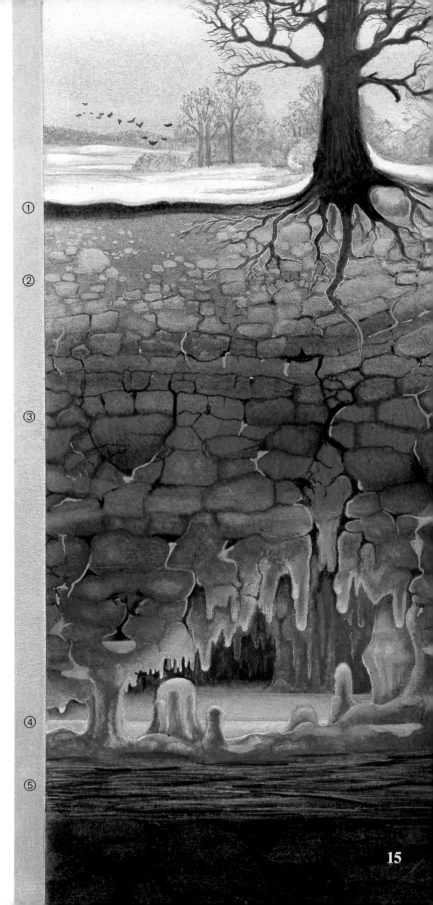

15

Plants and Roots

As the spring arrives, plants and animals that have been resting in the earth all winter are beginning to show signs of life.

At the edges of the woods, it is already quite warm. The beech seed (1) has survived the ice and frost, hidden under dried leaves and protected by its hard skin. Now the beechnut starts to sprout. Gravity guides the roots deeper into the earth.

The earth holds the plants' network of roots firmly. This is important for tall trees. Their roots grow many feet down, searching for water.

Plants take the water they need from the soil. If the soil is dry, their roots have to grow deep down to reach moisture. Just behind the tip of every root is a fuzz of delicate root hairs. You can see them enlarged in the center picture (2).

The root hairs are like thousands of tiny drinking straws which suck up the water. Lots of the soil's minerals are dissolved in this water. Plants need minerals to grow. The leaves and flowers grow up, against gravity.

The beech seedling can easily push through the dead leaves on the ground. But it isn't as easy for all plants. Deep in the soil the snowdrop (3) grows two strong leaves from its bulb. They push through the earth with their hard edges. The white flower is protected between the leaves.

The wood anemone (4) grows with its stem bent in a loop. It pulls its leaves and flowers up behind it so that they won't be damaged. The sturdy leaves of the butterbur (5) protect the young flower as it makes its way up through the soil.

At this time of year there is often a cold wind which shakes and tears at the new spring flowers. But their roots hold them firmly in the soil and they soon unfold their flowers in the warm sun.

The bumblebee (6) feeds on plant nectar. Then it flies in zigzags low over the ground. It is looking for a hole to start a new bumblebee colony. The brimstone butterfly (7) has also awakened and is fluttering along the edge of the wood. The badger (8) snuffles into view at the entrance to its **sett** (burrow). It won't look for food until it gets dark.

17

Underground Nests

Spring is a good time for young animals to be born. Their parents can find plenty of food for them. Many young animals grow up under the ground, hidden and safe from their enemies. (These underground nests are not as close together as they look in the picture).

The field mouse (1) has just heard a suspicious noise. It quickly carries its young into a second hole. It always keeps a hideaway ready in case of danger.

The eggs of the kingfisher (2) also hatch underground, usually in the river bank. The chicks sit in a hollow at the end of a long tunnel and wait for their parents to come back with small fish for them to eat. The chick nearest the entrance will have this mouthful. Then they all move around one place so that each chick is fed in turn.

Now that the sun has warmed the ground, the mole cricket (3) and beetle (4) can lay their eggs in the earth. The ants (5) have left their nest to look for food.

The bumblebee (6) has built its honeycomb in an old mouse nest. It is now queen of a bumblebee colony. Lots of worker bumblebees grew from its first eggs. They will collect pollen and nectar from the spring flowers to take back to the honeycomb. Some of it will be used to feed the new bumblebee larvae. The rest will be stored as honey for cold rainy days.

Deep below the roots is a rabbit burrow (7). Only the mother and two of her young are left in this nest. The other young rabbits must be exploring the entrance to the burrow. They want to go out into the meadow.

19

Earthworms and Other Earth Workers

When the damp earth begins to steam in the sunshine, many of the small animals living in the top layer of soil become more active.

The common earthworm starts to burrow through the soil, eating earth as it goes. The earthworm feeds on the plants in the earth. All the food which it can't digest is passed out as worm casts (1).

The earthworm is a **hermaphrodite**. That means that it is both male and female at the same time.

When two worms have fertilized each other (2) they can each lay a lot of tiny eggs (3). Each egg is wrapped in a blob of jelly. After three to four weeks, a worm may hatch out of the egg.

During the night the earthworm often brings home leaves and dried grass (4) for its food store. If you shine a flashlight at the worm, it will hurry back into its hole. The earthworm doesn't have any eyes but it can tell when it is light. Each segment on the worm's slimy body is sensitive to the light. The worm can't breathe if it dries out in the sun.

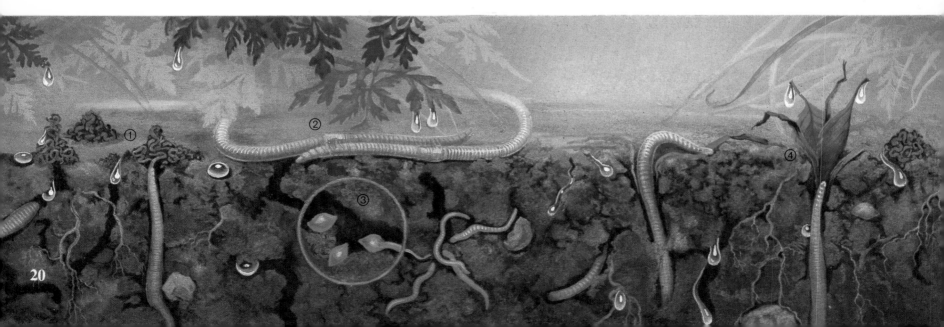

This blackbird knows how to trick the worm out of its hiding place in good weather. The blackbird hops up and down on the ground. The worm thinks that the vibrations in the soil are raindrops splashing on the ground so it comes out. The blackbird has food for its two chicks (5).

Other animals eat worms too. The hedgehog (6), the common toad (7), the starling (8), and the brass beetle (9) all eat worms. Even underground, worms have to escape from the mole (10) and field shrew (11) which will eat them.

A millipede (18) has rolled itself up and is pretending to be dead. You might see a wolf spider with its eggs (19). If you were to look through a magnifying glass you would see even smaller animals, like springtails (20) or mites (21).

Millions of fungi, algae, bacteria, and single cell animals (22) live there quite invisible to us. It was once calculated that in a handful of soil from the woods, there are more living things than there are people on earth.

As they burrow, the earthworms help to break up the soil. This lets air and water reach the plants' roots more easily. Worm casts are good for the soil, too, as they contain valuable minerals.

Push aside some old leaves and you will see lots of animals rush away from the light. A ground beetle (12) scuttles away frightened. An earwig (13) tries to crawl back into the dark earth. Ants (14), a geophilus (15), a woodlouse (16), and a centipede (17) are all scurrying around.

1	Worm casts	12	Ground beetle
2	Two worms fertilize each other	13	Earwig
3	Earthworm eggs (enlarged)	14	Ants
4	Earthworm getting food	15	Geophilus
5	Blackbird with two chicks	16	Woodlouse
6	Hedgehog	17	Centipede
7	Common toad	18	Millipede
8	Starling	19	Wolf spider with eggs
9	Brass beetle	20	Springtail
10	Mole	21	Mite
11	Field shrew	22	Invisible earth workers

Plant and Animal Communities

In the summer, the countryside has a thick covering of bushes, grasses and flowers. The soil underneath is well protected. The leaves shade the earth and the roots keep the earth firm. The covering of plants protects the earth from being blown away by the wind or washed away by the rain.

If you have ever picked a bunch of wild flowers you will know that there are lots of different kinds. You won't find the same kinds of flowers growing in woods as you will find on hillsides.

Each plant can only grow where it has everything it needs to live. Some plants need sunshine, other plants need shade, or a lot of moisture. Each plant needs particular minerals from the soil.

◀ Plant and animal communities in fields which are regularly plowed and cultivated.

1 Common poppy
2 Wild mustard
3 Field penny-cress
4 Field pansy
5 Honeybee
6 Large white butterfly

Plant and ▶ animal communities in the shade at the edge of woods and fields. Here the soil is moist and nutritional.

1 Common nettle
2 Cow parsley
3 Common sorrel
4 Tortoiseshell butterfly with caterpillars
5 Soldier beetle
6 Leaf-eating beetle

22

There are some plants which need lime in the soil. Some plants can only grow in rich, nutritional soil, while others can survive in poorer soil.

Many plants with the same needs live in the same place and make up a community. You can tell what the soil is like by the plants which are growing in it. The pictures on these pages show just four of the possible plant and animal communities.

Unfortunately, a lot of wild flowers are killed as weeds. Others die because their soil has been drained for farming. Some plants can no longer find the right soil to grow in and are almost extinct. Animals are threatened too, as many of them depend on these plants for food and shelter.

◀ Plant and animal communities in damp fields or near streams. Here the soil contains a lot of water.

Plant and ▶ animal communities at the edge of fields and roads. Here the soil is warm, dry and contains lime.

1 Cabbage thistle
2 Ragged robin
3 Water avens
4 Marsh marigold
5 Water forget-me-not
6 Dragonfly
7 Mayfly

1 Trembling grass
2 Meadow sage
3 Field scabious
4 Bladder campion
5 Ox-eye daisy
6 Lady's bedstraw
7 Common blue butterfly

Natural Habitats

Plants and animals need a place to live and grow. But it can't be just any place. Each different plant and animal has its own natural habitat.

The dandelion doesn't need a lot of space to grow above the ground. But its roots need a firm hold in earth where it can find food.

The mole's habitat is underground. It sleeps in its nest and looks for worms and insects in its underground tunnels. The mounds of earth in the meadow show that its living area is about 30–60 feet long and about as wide. A lot of moles often live in the same field, but they each have their own **territory**. Sometimes there is a quarrel where two boundaries meet as you can see in the picture.

Fights are rare, though, as the animals have lots of other ways to look after their territory. The fox urinates like a dog on trees and bushes. The smell is a warning sign for other foxes: Stop, another fox lives here! A fox's territory has to be about the size of two or three football fields so that it can find enough to eat on its night raids.

Deer usually live in small groups. On summer evenings they come out from the woods where they live to eat in the fields. But the deer, like many other animals, are losing their natural habitats, as woods are cut down and land is used to build roads and houses.

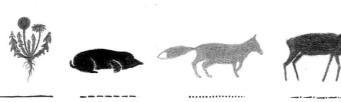

| Dandelion | Mole | Fox | Deer |

1 Horse
2 Stag
3 Deer
4 Wild boar
5 Common hare
6 Fox
7 Cat
8 Long-tailed field mouse
9 Tree frog

10 Grasshopper
11 Millipede
12 Adder
13 Slug
14 Mole
15 Earthworm
16 Swallow
17 Dragonfly
18 Large white butterfly

Moving Around

Have you ever seen a mole flying through the air? Or a swallow burrowing in the earth? Of course not. Each animal is adapted to its own living space and moves around there in its own way.

The millipede bustles away on its 200 tiny legs. But a lot of animals can move about without feet. The snake slithers along in supple coils. The slug can crawl over even the sharpest obstacle on its slimy track without hurting itself.

The horse is well equipped to move around on firm ground. When it's hungry, it puts one foot in front of the other as it grazes. When there is any sign of danger, it gallops away at great speed. Stags and deer need to be able to do this too.

There are animals moving around in the ground as well as on the ground. The mole pushes the earth to one side with its strong digging feet. The earthworm stretches its body and then squashes it up behind. It has tiny bristles on its skin to help it grip the earth and move along.

The common hare hops across the field and then zigzags back to confuse the chasing fox. The cat stalks silently through the grass on its padded paws. But the mouse scurries quickly away. The tree frog and grasshopper spring out of the way with their long back legs, just as the enemy pounces.

Above the ground, swallows, dragonflies and butterflies are flying in the air. But they also need space on the ground, or at least on a tree, so that they can rest for a while.

Food from the Soil

In the autumn, farmers can begin to harvest the potato fields. In the picture you can see a seed potato which was planted in the spring. During the summer, a potato plant grew from the seed potato. Roots grew downward and the stem and leaves, with their pale lilac flowers and green fruit, grew above the ground.

Underground, a lot of new potatoes began to grow on long shoots from the seed potato. Each new potato is full of nutrients. The new potatoes will provide the potato plant with food next spring. But the farmer will dig up some of the potatoes so that we can eat the potato plant's food store too.

A long time ago, people learned how to grow plenty of food from a few seeds. That was the beginning of agriculture. Once the seeds have been planted, the growing plants have to be protected against an army of pests. The colorado beetle (1), its larvae (2) and lots of small animals and diseases can destroy the harvest.

After the harvest the field is plowed so that air can get into the soil. The plants have taken a lot of nutrients out of the ground so the farmer replaces them with a fertilizer. Next year he will plant a different crop in the field so that the soil won't lose the same nutrients all the time and become infertile.

Farmers all over the world hope there will be enough rain and sun for the plants to grow and ripen properly. Otherwise their crops fail. In some parts of the world there is not enough fertile soil to grow food. In desert areas and in the mountains, people often go hungry.

In this country we can grow enough food in the spring and summer to be able to store food for the winter. Animals must store food for the winter too. Some have to eat as much food as they can in the autumn and store it as fat under their skins.

②

Renewing the Soil

During the last warm days of autumn the gold beech leaves float slowly down to the ground. Soon the weather gets colder and the wind pulls the last leaves from the branches.

Dead leaves and withered plants pile up on the ground every autumn. Some animals also die, like the greenfinch in the picture (1).

What happens to everything that has died? It is eaten. Millions of small animals feed on the dead plants and animals. These are the animals that live in the soil. (Look back to page 21.)

All these animals eat different things. Some, like the burying beetle (2) or the maggots of the greenbottle fly (3), eat dead animals. The horn of plenty (4) and other fungi feed on decaying leaves and dead wood. Tiny bacteria, algae, and single cell animals make the leaves moist and tender so that the woodlice (5), millipedes (6), earthworms (7), and other animals can eat them.

You may think that animals which eat dead things are disgusting. But without them the earth would have been buried under mountains of waste long ago. These tiny animals are called **decomposers** because they help change all the dead things into crumbly black earth. Gardeners can see this happening in their compost heaps. Decomposers turn plant and kitchen waste into new, fertile soil called **humus**.

All these animals living in the soil are important because they break down almost all the dead things into tiny parts. Some of these will be minerals. In the picture these are shown as stars. Let's see what happens to them.

The Mineral Cycle

Just imagine that the star (1) is a mineral or some other nutrient important for plants. It has been in the ground for a long time. One day the rain water takes it to the roots of the beech tree.

The roots suck up the mineral in the water and the mineral becomes part of the tree's sap (2). As the sap rises, it carries the mineral through the tree trunk toward the end of a branch. There the beech uses the mineral as an important part of a beechnut (3). The beechnut grows and, in the autumn, falls to the ground.

A long tailed field mouse gnaws at the beechnut (4). Now the field mouse stores the mineral in its body. The mouse is eaten by a marten (5). But the marten dies too.

Now the decomposers take over (6). They break down the dead animal, so the mineral is back in the ground. It can be taken up once again by a plant.

Many plants however, are not eaten by an animal. They die and go directly to the decomposers in the ground. You can see in the picture how the mineral then follows a smaller circle (7). It goes constantly from living things back into the earth. Otherwise the soil's store of minerals would have been used up long ago.

The same star has been on its journey for millions of years. But just imagine if the star were a poison. Some pollutants can be carried through air and into the soil in water. The plants would take up the poison and pass it on until, finally, it would end up back in the soil. It could be passed on to people through food growing in the soil. This is why we have to be careful not to pollute the soil.

The Sleeping Earth

The winter countryside is quiet and deserted. The ground is under a deep layer of snow. Here and there some tracks in the snow show that there are still some animals around. Many of the animals have found safe hiding places in the ground for the winter.

The snow keeps the earth warm, like the blankets on a bed. Where there is no snow, the frost can reach 20–30 inches deep. This doesn't bother the mole (1) at all. If the cold reaches its nest, the mole just moves deeper into the earth.

The mole's food store is sometimes full of earthworms. They won't escape because the mole has bitten them so that they can't move. Otherwise they would burrow deeper like the earthworm in the picture (2). It has lined a little hollow with slime and has rolled up tightly to sleep through the winter. The common dormouse (3) snuggles down under dry leaves. It will sleep until next spring.

The dormouse can live on the fat it stored up in the autumn when it ate a lot of nuts. The badger (4) sleeps deep down in its sett. It only has to go out into the ice and snow occasionally for food.

Like so many plants and animals, we depend on the earth for our food. This is why it is important that we do not pollute the soil or waste the earth's precious resources.

Index